To Tu... nia

there is an england

Best wishes

Harry Gallagher

Harry Gallagher

Stairwell Books //

Published by Stairwell Books
161 Lowther Street
York, YO31 7LZ

www.stairwellbooks.co.uk
@stairwellbooks

ISBN: 978-1-913432-57-7
p5

Cover art: Roz Gadd, with the technical assistance of Jade Gadd
www.rozgadd.co.uk

Also by Harry Gallagher

Northern Lights

"For Noah Lively, Reuben Lively & Jack Richardson –
boys of today, men of tomorrow."

Table of Contents

Introduction	1
Acknowledgements	2
there is an england	3
Home	5
The Girl Who Turned into a Cormorant	7
Mining for Sweetness	8
Youth Training	9
Arthur Wharton's Dream	10
Longview	11
St Joan of the Waves	12
Tinnitus Express	13
The Universe Exhales	14
Nasa Announces the Discovery of Water on the Moon	15
Old Rudeboy	16
Red Squirrel	17
Parkhour	18
'Savages'	19
Shipyard Blues	20
Hope Stones	21
'Funny'	22
Flown	24
Hughie	26
The Dredging of Bluebird	27
6.30am BC	28
In The Stars	29
Things I Learned During a Pandemic	30
The Children of Albion	31
Perfidia	33
Breathless	34
Bullybird	35
Behind Grey Eyes on a Rush Hour Tube Train	36
Everyday Miracles	37
NHS at Christmas	38
Mr Robeson Sings for His Supper	39
As If the Old Man	40
Coughing Fog on the Road	41

Clutching at Dreams 42
Fox Rocks 43
Folk Club 44
Send Us... 45
From Peterloo to Tolpuddle 46
Tale of the Riverbank 47
Mr Byrne 48
The Ambling, the Dancing 49
You Do Not Speak for Me 50
The Dreams of an Everyday Teenaged Boy 52
Friday Night Rehearsal 53
Session 54
Training 55
Desiderata 56
New Town, Old Story 57
Sing 58
Imago 60
A Warming Lullaby 61
A Frayed Reassurance 62
Never Go Home 63
Bluesky Thinking 64
Instructions for Would-Be Poets 65
Surf's Up 67
Doorstepping / Goosestepping 68
Love in Winter 69
Goodnight from Mars 70
Whisperfish 71
Advice to Children 72
Commence the Dancing... 73
Dot....dot....dot.... 74
Boiling a Frog 75
Waiting for the Swallows' Return 76
Midmorning Springtown 77
Echoes 79
What We Have Become 80
Not Rain 81
Song of the Six Million 82
'Unskilled' 84
Island 86

Happy Yet?   87
Meeting Male Audience Members After Poetry Readings 88
The Queen of Lost Things   90
The God of Perfect Things   91
We Are Each Other   93

Introduction

This collection of poems was written between 2016 and 2021, a period of huge social change for one of the richest nations in the world. A country with a parliament dating back over 800 years, a country which boasts a long line of engineers, inventors and pioneers who between them nigh-on made the modern world as we know it. Yet it was also a country which – to the eyes of many outsiders – seemed hell-bent on a level of self-harm which many of its inhabitants would previously never have believed possible.

Central to this state of affairs was, it seemed obvious to the author, that England has misplaced its sense of identity. Who is it? What does it stand for? What is its place in the world? Add to this mix a pandemic whose effect on the lives of all UK residents, not to say most people on the planet, was to further isolate them from each other.

At the time of writing, the way ahead is unclear. The UK is out of the European Union, having been led to believe Europe and outsiders generally were to blame for our lack of confidence in our own identity. England particularly led the way in voting 'Out', Scotland having singularly done the opposite, but nevertheless having to leave at the behest of its somewhat dominant neighbour.

The UK as a union now appears under greater threat than at any time in living memory, all the while the gap between the haves and have-nots growing ever wider.

This collection does not attempt to provide all, or indeed any solutions to the above conundrums – that's not the mission of poetry. Instead, it paints a picture of what life was like for ordinary English people, how it was in the past and is now. In that sense, it's not overarchingly political.

Instead, it generally leans toward the personal, weaving in and out of timelines and locations to portray the ins and outs of everyday life in England, then and now. It is, more than anything else, a plea for its people to have an intelligent, informed conversation and recognise that the things which made the nation great – a sense of fair play, decency and tolerance – are worth far more than seem currently fashionable.

Acknowledgements

A few of these poems first appeared in Orbis, Prole, Atrium, The New European and North East Bylines.

there is an england

there is an england
of sycamore trees
dappled in sunlight
their dalmation leaves
standing guard over verges

of ginnels between houses
whose doors bear a welcome,
kettles ever bubbling,
sofas ever dented from
shared laughter at daftness

of ice cream vans
tinkling their way through
the 99 dreams
and the skipping of children,
fists full of piggybank raidings

of dads with tall tales
for wideopen little ears,
their secret codes
of clicks and winks
velcro for wonderment

of bus drivers dispensing
directions like boiled sweets
to confused old wayfarers
in the marathon weave between
bellringing and the door

of post office clerks'
fascination and patience
at a pensioner's to-do list
exchanged like currency,
new pennies for gold nuggets

of pub quizzers pondering
that one crucial question
they'll have forgotten when
asked in the morning, wiped
like brows at chuckingout time

of handholding old couples,
ramblers, amblers, schoolteachers,
cookingfat splashed forearms
wrapping lunch in fish and chip
paper gone stale, unread

there is an england
in streetlights and shadows,
in terraces and shops
open hands bearing chipped mugs of tea,
extra biscuits for pilgrims. ⁂

Home

It's in the puddlesoaked face
of the old sparrow watcher
as it pecks incessant
at the porous mortar
which is holding the bricks
of his existence together.

It's in the jingle of children
skipping home from school,
who fancies who
ringing in the air
as they firstfoot new ways
to live in their own skin.

It's in the cataracted memories
of oldmen and women,
as hazy as haar
rolling in from the sea,
the days and weeks playing out,
set to gently repeat.

It's underwear on washing lines
brightening back yards,
new life forcing its way
through paving stone cracks,
the swoop and attack
of a newly written melody.

It's crumbs left on the lawns
of public parks by old soldiers
who have nothing else to do
except feed the pigeons
so swear an oath
to keep looking up.

It's pension day post offices,
queues outside before 9,
library books returned late,
the fine taken in the form
of an exchange of warmth,
time spent is not wasted.

It's the taste of the sea,
the sneeze of cutgrass,
the blaze of the sun,
the jag of the northwind
bringing you up short
just to remind you you're home. //

The Girl Who Turned into a Cormorant

The redhaired girl with cormorant eyes
is spying the tide, an offing in mind,
her Viking blood oiling the wings
waiting at her back for a windchange.

The loping old seadog serves Sunday
coffees from a hatch, his faraway look
casting back to catches he landed
before his rusty hip called it a day.

Thugdog lad, his threat on a leash
teeth sharp asa shark straining for flesh,
puts his pride in its bite, as he once might
have done hot rivets caught by his grandad.

The redhaired girl looks back just once.
She's seen old snaps of beaming flatcaps
standing proud by halibut big asa boxer,
fuel for families flocked to the dockside.

Bold as the seabird she is,
she follows tomorrow,
feels the pull of the tide,
opens her wings and flies. ⁄⁄

Mining for Sweetness

Tiptoeing in the pantry of my memory
I can see him asif the light were still on,
his work-eaten thoughts all full up,
rummaging hungry in Winter's gloom.

His oilblack prints fingered the gold,
glistening in the seam of a deepcut shelf.
All restraint flown away like tinfoil in a gale.
Look, kids! I've found some candies!

The rush to the well of utter perfection
was on before the boss could intervene.
We tore in, oblivious to the pressure's hiss.
You stupid bugger, they were for Christmas!

When I picture him now he's deep in that mine
full of adventure and picking like mad,
turning up trinkets to light up little faces,
digging for Christmases he never had. ⁄⁄

Youth Training

Fifty apple green Summers ago
there lived a boy who
by some it was said
was easily led.

Whose mischievous sisters,
tall tale tellers both,
one day convinced him,
picked him up and rinsed him,
that if he closed his wide eyes
and steamtrained a woo-hoo!
smoke would blow out
of his unfilled ears.

His fears of ridicule,
well-founded it seems,
were waved away by the sisters –
he was Jack with the beans!

The Mockery Express
stopped at all stations.

But on misty winter nights,
leaves strewn across the four-foot,
beneath dimming streetlights,
he smells the coal, smells the soot.

Hears the stoker's steel shovel
scrape the footplate of his mind.
Eyes closed, woo-hooing.
Smoke every time. ⁄⁄

Arthur Wharton's Dream

From a scorched Gold Coast
to standing still between sticks
on icy Yorkshire nights,
Arthur Wharton looks upfield
at a sunnier future.

One where picking brickbats
from his overstretched net
is a memory faded,
waned like touchlines
on longlost pitches.

A century and a half
of tiny babysteps
and such a long, long way to go. ⫻

Longview

The North, chipped and scavenged
in these standing stone days,
does not fall asunder
nor domino down
in sight of barber surgeons
with their slingshots, chippings.

Long abraded by high seas,
we stack lean as limestone,
holding our breath
like we have held our noses,
impassive in the face
of this flitting ephemera.

We Danelaw children,
sons and daughters of the trod,
are forged from such stuff
as cannot be dreamt of.
Today or tomorrow,
hope will prevail. ⁄⁄

St Joan of the Waves

Combing the sands, she scans for bottletops,
sweetie wrappers, seaglass. Her mineral eyes
keen asa whetted breeze, pick between litter
for the lost, the hopeless, the cracked castoffs.

Wading shameless in her knickers, her flying
skirt – a gull over the waves – is a handkerchief
mopping up oldmen's eyes, who walked to
water's edge wondering when or if they'd stop.

She picks them all up, dabs their stories dry
with the touch of a mother, picks up a pen
and writes. ⁄⁄

Tinnitus Express

The train currently squealing into platform 1
is the 4.15am express service to Tinnitus.
We regret that there is no further sleep on board,
the sharp steel wheels being in a particularly bad mood
due to the lack of soft damp leaves on the line.

There are no quiet carriages on today's service
but you can listen to your own onboard selection
of dentistry drills, old fax machines and white noise.
This train calls at all stations and never terminates. ⁄⁄

The Universe Exhales

Time brushes the sand
with the soft of its palm,
its fingernails scratching
at the old harbour wall.

Dogs chase tennis balls,
at their masters' whim,
jumping the waves
and failing majestic.

Clans chat at a distance,
their frets and their woes
and disbelief baptised in
the clean air between them.

The universe exhales,
its shallow breath catching
everyone we ever knew
in a tender cosmic flash. ⫽

Nasa Announces the Discovery of Water on the Moon

We're off to find Baby Clanger
thriving in the moon's abyssal,
my 50-year-old spacesuit
is off its coat hanger,
I've dusted off my Swanee whistle.

I'll gurgle at the Soup Dragon,
all crinkly at the seams
and blow a kiss alltheway
back down to the earth
on the cheek of boyhood dreams. ⟁

Old Rudeboy

He is an old rudeboy,
skintight and neat,
size 11 Docs
on size 8 feet.
Specials and Selecter
playing on repeat,
moonstomping while chomping
on an old boiled sweet.

He is an old rudeboy
swaggering up my street,
the actual article
from the original elite,
Ben Sherman and Sta-press
strutting to the Beat,
stopping for a breather
in the afternoon heat.

An old rudeboy,
crombie not an inch too long,
head shave no longer needed
but the beat goes on and on. //

Red Squirrel

The dominion of the North Country King
is a shrunken wild but still as wide
as the eye can spy in these forever days,
with blackberries shining their rubies,
pearling by the river's thrum.

By rule of thumb, he'll be hereabouts,
poised to spring at the corner of the eye
of some random passer-by,
a regal flash, dashing through
the picture's frame, keeping the flame
of Old England alight. ⁄⁄

Parkhour

The redhaired girl
marching in the park
hup two, hup two
against the clock
ticking steady in her head
swings past the roundabout.
Record time again,
everyday a winner.

The pufferjacket couple,
steps asymmetrical,
are trying hard to think
of words to warm the air
hanging frozen between them.
The day being out of step,
they sit and balance out a bench.

The shaggy, soggy dog,
wild with the wind,
bounds around the bins.
Its owner, running sorry,
replays childhood memories
of chasing tousled pigeons,
always one hop out of reach.

As mud and mulch settle,
the sky sends down a feather
which waltzes on the wind,
landing softly in the tundra
between the glassy lovers.

They tightrope across
and meet in the middle. //

'Savages'

*"THE MISSING LINK: A creature manifestly between the
gorilla and the Negro is to be met within some of the lowest
districts of London and Liverpool by adventurous explorers.
It comes from Ireland, whence it has contrived to migrate; it
belongs in fact to a tribe of Irish savages: the lowest species
of Irish Yahoo. When conversing with its kind it talks a sort
of gibberish. It is, moreover, a climbing animal, and may
sometimes be seen ascending a ladder laden with a hod of
bricks."*
Punch Magazine, London, 1862

Savages, they're callin' us,
for we work on hill and dell,
but our children are not cast down
into Old Nick's pits of Hell.

We breathe in The Lord's pure air,
are washed clean by Heaven's rain
an' we eat an' drink the fruits
of the blessed barley grain.

In houses set from mud an' stone
we raise our clans as best we can,
though not so well as in the sooted slums
favoured by the Englishman,

who bathes in vats of money
from his coalmine an' his mill,
where he mangles man an' boy alike,
slaves to their master's will.

An' now they drive us from our homes,
laws sprung up at their command.
God save us from the Englishman
an' his blight upon our land. ✍

Shipyard Blues

Steamhammer Sammy
loves his lass an' bairns an' that
but it'd take the chains
sleepin' on the slipway
to pull it out of him
an' anyway they already know.

Flyboy Frankie
is brewin' up in the cabin.
He's not the quickest
but he knows well the whistle
an' the drummin' of boots
towards tea in tin mugs.

Big Col the caulker,
one hand almighty,
can already picture it
grippin' a pintglass
but right now cannat feel
the sugar soap's scour.

The Ship In The Hole's bar
is lined with full marble glasses
all waitin' for the buzzer
to let out the welders,
the painters, the scaffs
from the Hell that they have come to love.

   * * *

Timeslip Tommy,
Section Leader of White Goods,
sniffs at sales of fridges made
in a land oceans away.
He feels he is missing something
but that ship has long sailed. ∥

20

Hope Stones

Hope stones on the clifftops
for when blackcloud descends,
posing as a staircase,
its icy bannister melting
all the long drop down.

Skyblue energy pebbles,
Heaven's berries,
sweet as life, say
Stick around kid,
I love you.

Imagine a world where
every thoroughfare
is lined with hope stones,
handpainted in the minutes
between juggling life's skittles.
We could pick up and replace –
little filling-up stations.

Just picture the difference!
Taking the knee
to view the wideworld
from someone else's angle,
eachtime rising refilled
to rethink, rebuild. ⟋⟋

'Funny'

The sticky sickly stench
of schoolhall floors
lurches like a kicked horse
in the unstable pit
of an ageing memory.

Sweat glands earn their keep,
digging snowdrift deep
to the ill-fitting mumble,
soon to be leaver
of a mockery of a school,
about to be mocked
before mucking up his exams.

The Head Of English rises,
laurel just off stage right,
waxes on and on unlyrical
about his little disappointments
and how here's a prime example.

The boy-shambles' surname
sergeant-majors from the stage
and he stands up on parade,
a single reddening face
in a company of two hundred
and his feathery essay,
a paperweight already,
is dissected asif by hamfingers
overly fond of scissors.

Is this supposed to be funny son?
draws sniggers from the stalls,
each one secretly relieved
to still be a bum on a seat.

I sat back down
and veryquickly faded
unqualified from school,
serenaded by surprise
and isn't it a shame,
all my foolish noodlings
neatly folded up and fed
into our coalfire's flames.

I wasn't his son
and he wasn't my dad.
My dad kept sharp tools
well away from his kids. ⁄⁄

Flown

Was it Peter or Joey?
Time has feathered away
the fluttering details,
but in the midst of a day
just like any other
the voice of my nana
spoke clear to my mother,
not from the cold earth,
but from a budgerigar,
perky on its perch.

On her last balmy afternoons,
the old girl had passed the hours
by passing words to a bird
like the fading flowers
now wilted atop
the stone on her plot.

The bird, in turn
passed on, rehoused,
spoke up and returned
the old lady's voice
across the living room
at the ears of her daughter,
like a wrong 'un from
a wily spin bowler.

Asif instead of having a fall
and fading slowly away,
in the midst of a day
just like any other
she had flown the cage
of her council flat,
clad in the plumage

of a tiny wee mimic
with sensitive ears,
a time machine
and a penchant for tears. ⁄⁄

Hughie

Such a little face to have
the world writ large on it.
Hands-in-pockets bowed head walk,
rain and sun bouncing off
round shoulders just the same.

An old man by my time, Hughie.
Bent as beaten iron
in the glory of the flame,
fingers fat with graft,
yellowed from the woodbine tabs
with occasional burns when you
drew them down to the bone.

Just a jig between the cracks
of time, waltzing back
to the wife they all said
had kept you in check,
when she wasn't setting light
to the rest of the world.

But the times I saw you lit up,
it was all in the re-telling
of a thousand hungry days.
You, wiry as a coat hanger
in a cold empty wardrobe,
cap on the floor, you were
back on the pavement.

Eighty going on twenty,
singing for your supper,
your dinner, your tea.
A shrug and a wink,
nowt too proper,
happy as a cornerboy
with a capful of copper. ⁄⁄

The Dredging of Bluebird

I was there that day
when they pulled you from the lake,
bones inside a burntblack corpse.

The son of a father,
another obsessed, ended smashed up,
Godsped down, down to the depths.

Flash forward thirty years,
sunnyday tourists gawp
from a paddle steamer's face.

Their captain asides,
"Oh and there on the left"
(a momentary murmur)

"under tarpaulin and sludge,
they're dredging up
the heft of Bluebird".

Boys race to their dads
with the breaking news.
First to tell wins approval ⁄⁄

6.30am BC

Do magpies know they sound like
velociraptors from Jurassic Park?
Clacking at eachother over stretches
of temporarily tamed suburban savannahs,
talons pin down helpless crusts
taken stillwarm from bird tables.

From the corner of the shot,
mug of tea in hand, a tyrannosaur
yawns and the plains are cleared. ⁄⁄

In The Stars

Contrary to perceived wisdom
(if you can call it that),
the sun doesn't revolve around us
and the earth was never flat.

It's folly that the Wall of China
can be viewed from space.
Orion has no belt to buckle,
the moon doesn't possess a face.

The stars can't tell your future,
though read them if you must;
today's horoscope will never say
Tomorrow you will be dust.

Seeing faces in the fire
and ourselves up in the sky,
merely ways to make some sense
of the days before we die.

Yet every human who ever lived
has gazed at that same nightsky
and had to pause to dab away
something suddenly in their eye.

Raging untamed, undimming, wild,
this tiny corner of Time
hides secrets in its pockets
to save our fragile minds.

Seven billion little people
scrabbling for food and ground
might see how very small we are
if we looked up instead of around. ⁂

Things I Learned During a Pandemic

There can be sanctuary in silence.

A smile from a passing stranger
encountered in a sunny hour
catches faster than any virus.

The plainest birds
have all the best songs.

An unused playground
can be the saddest sight.

Saying thank you together
is balm for the soul.

Little boys can fight viruses
with stories and wooden swords.

The people who matter,
who keep us alive
and on who we depend
are never politicians.

The media is not your friend.

A computer screen contains nothing
to rival a hug.

Community leaves its doors unlocked
and shouts across the street
to see how you're doing for milk.

Your grown up children
wear their kindnesses lightly,
as they tend to the ailing
and carry your pride everyday. ⚘

The Children of Albion

The children of Albion
maraud at the seaside,
smashedup vodka bottles
spray sharp wet confetti
for virgin flesh to find.

The Sunday morning talk
outside St George's church
is of young 'uns these days,
how they're feral and fierce
and bring back the birch.

How they come around here
leaving their shit for
decent people to pick up;
how they need a good kicking
and how a bloody good clip
never did us any harm,
we good people of England,
full of indignation,
dishing out retribution
in some dark torture chamber
of our dotaged dreams.

But the children of Albion
are English to their bones,
poor bastard progeny
of the furiously feudal,
these done-tos and havenots
filledup on futureless cornflakes
from Aldi and Lidl,
while their paylords and masters
flick them the fingers
from the breakfast tables
of touchless towers.

So the children of Albion
seethe to the seaside
(as soon as they're allowed),
offer prayers up to Churchill,
give thanks to The Few,
piss on pictures of Germans,
sing brave songs to England
and her Empire-building slaves,
whose shadows will on
the incoming waves. ⁄⁄

Perfidia

Mr Robson says thank you for
the flags and street parties
he could hear if his window
in the last room along
wasn't screwed down.

Ruth misses her fiancé,
who went off to the desert
and returned, but not really.
Her lovely boy brought back
a lifetime of fury and drink.

Hugh is refusing this morning
to answer to his name. He says
he is not in the mood to listen
to junior ranks eager to go home
to their barbecues and bunting.

Mary Anne says the cake
baked just now in the kitchen
by a young care assistant
reminds her of her mummy
and begins to cry.

In the residents lounge they are
all ever so grateful for
Glenn Miller playing on loop.
Doors locked, they hum to Perfidia,
its meaning burning like bullets. ⁄⁄

Breathless

The bonobo says hello
and would politely like to know
what happened to its forest,
caught up in the crossfire
of someone else's war.

The orangutan wonders
could anyone disclose
the meaning of 'critical',
as her home is bulldozed
to print up reports,
so the ape who walks upright
can wring its soiled hands
before washing them
and sleeping sound at night.

The blue whale, slow,
seemingly unenthusiastic,
unlocks its trawler mouth
and fills up on plastic,
its great placid brain
composing a refrain
as sad and deep as
blanched coral seabeds.

In highrise conurbations
of over developed nations
foreign trips are cancelled
for a one-off blip,
a sour aberration.
A major spike downwards
but just a minor setback
on a vile wallgraph
of the longterm plan
to continually expand
until the whole wide world
gasps breathless. //

Bullybird

Here comes the bullybird;
blackhearted, hooded,
shocking blue coat
shown off like a hunting cup.

Chest puffed and sheened,
he gleans the shiny things
from the shabbylife nests
of the smallest birds,
wafts of jetsam and toil
slandering his air.

Here comes the bullybird,
scene-stealing fence sitter,
shitting down the blindside
while sitting pretty, adored.

Raucous toned, drunk on protection,
he struts through the lights
down to the apron,
allthewhile preening
through the flashlamp moments
of a vainglorious life.

Here comes the bullybird,
feinting one way,
swooping the other
and the silence inside him
roars loud as oceans. ⌁

Behind Grey Eyes on a Rush Hour Tube Train

Eyes, I know you of old;
ragged and baggy,
empty as dustbins,
galvanized and clanking,
lidless, hopeless.

Roundshouldered as a tor
on a long rainyday,
grainy as black'n'white
films on a Sunday;
nicotined, captured,
no happy ending.

Suited and booted
but the solitary tramlines
run clean through your hope,
your overtime scheme
that became a necessity,
a rentman's wet dream.

Fourteen hour days,
sandwiched underground,
buttressed and crammed
as the fish in that mealbox
your mam used to pack.

You hear from her still
once a week on the phone:
Click your heels together love,
there's no place like home. //

Everyday Miracles

The diamond on Orion's shoulder
is fading fast as stars can move
and before we can correctly spell
'Betelgeuse', we will learn all about
real fireworks and how to say farewell.

Christopher setdown his love for Jean
on a gatepost in a field that felt
faroff from home, high in the sear of
a sixty-years-since Summer.
Now crowded out by a housing scheme,
their longkept secret is safe
from grandchildren's tired eyes,
which are fixed on a TV screen.

The wee seaside hamlet
surrenders its lovely jewels.
Buffed smooth by time and tide,
the furnaces' cast-offs
are presented with love
for wide eyes, soft fingers
and deep, damp pockets.

Every field, path, street corner
harbours stardust, twinkling unseen,
blushing among the grey and the green,
as we scurriers scratch livings,
pay our way as best we can,
raise our own tiny giants,
fall in love, fall apart,
look at each other
or nothing at all;
striding blind
through everyday miracles. ⁄⁄

NHS at Christmas

There are tears in the clinic as retinas detach,
scan shadows explained. There are moments profound,
tissues all round, talk of hope, coping strategies.

There are choices explored, stark asa pale wall
in a consulting office. Chemotherapy and barium
fill up conversational silence like so much lead.

There are loved ones holding hands, wondering who'll
be there to hold theirs at the end of the end,
when empty days will be enemies, never friends.

There are ladies with mops, skating around the dreams
of kiddies already half in Heaven and hush little baby
don't you cry, mummy's going to weep you a lullaby.

There are people waltzing out into the street,
light as prisoners newly released into freedom
and hope and tomorrows and tomorrows and tomorrows.

There are soft-voiced dominions who do not see dates,
only bodies, broken and bent. Through snow and sleep,
terrors and weeping, they wait faithful to mend. ⁄⁄

Mr Robeson Sings for His Supper

When Mr McCarthy's
witch-hunting was done,
an educated man, who grew
molasses in his chest
found himself suddenly
singing for his supper.

Every miner's club room,
each falldown village hall
shook with the shock
of the boom and croon,
as men with palms
that held up seam roofs
smacked them together
for a great whose face
looked just like theirs
coming out of the cage.

Now it seems, seams spent,
the spoil's grandchildren,
dazzled and blinded,
would call up the Klan,
hand over the man.

Ashfield, Bassetlaw,
Bury, Don Valley,
Keighley, Bolsover,
Bury and Blyth;
there's nought quite so black
as what we foster inside. ⫽

As If the Old Man

As if the old man, in dying,
had passed the boy a note
which looked for alltheworld
like Instructions For Living.

So the images began spilling,
raining through the ceiling
until the boy couldn't stop
them, even if he'd wanted to.

Robeson singing for his supper
in South Yorkshire village halls,
witch-hunted from his homeland
into the arms of soulbrothers.

How the keys to our shackles
were paid for by Tolpuddle.
Men who stood and said No!
We will, we will be free!

How the most swollen coffers
can be as cold and as empty
as deepspace, if not given
to the people who need it.

And how common decency is all.
How love can't always win out
but who would love a person
who floods the world with hate?

The boy pocketed the words deep
inside a favourite raincoat,
a reminder that fairer weather
is always around the corner. ⁄⁄

Coughing Fog on the Road

Settled like methane in the guts of a marsh,
smoke chokes the road, its breathless bedfellow.

Needling its way wicked down windpipes,
tattooing each lung: *Your tomorrows are mine.*

Night kidnaps the moon, smothering her smile
with the filthiest blanket from the old ICI,

tattered bluewave logo, a lunar chloroform cloth.
Sleepsound and dream now of penniless nightshifts

rattling like pebbles through the clanking shell
of evenings spent patching the arse pockets

of a people coughing up breakfast in bed
with bloody kisses on the cheek of Emphysema. ⁄⁄

Clutching at Dreams

The drunk woman sings,
a musical saw. Limbs
strong as rubberplants,
she bends unsteady,
arms clutching at dreams.

In this screech of a station
on a Friday night, she is
Whitney and Adele
and nobody need tell
her otherwise.

We all line the same
misty platform, each of us
lost in the fog
of who we think we are. ⁄⁄

Fox Rocks

Sleekit as greased wheels,
asa bluesman's dirty riff,
red as Ziggy's quiff,
I steal 'cross the road,
trailing brush as stiff
as a Gibson guitar
in the hands of Ronno,
The Stardust Kid.

A midnight shooting star,
I streak straight across
the desert of your eyes,
a rock'n'roll suicide.
But not quite tonight –
a few more licks
in the old dog yet. ⁄⁄

Folk Club

It's a dying art,
this communion.
In a slabcold room
we cluster for warmth,
serenade old comrades
fallen from the road,
sing our old songs,
each of us looking
a touch more worn
than last we checked.

Tentative as finches,
we reach for harmonies,
breadcrumbs, fairydust
we once took as ours.

Yet once in a while
a line winds its way
into a place,
deep and forgotten
asa memory of love.

Tearducts are squeezed,
soft peachy cheeks
dabbed with handkerchiefs
clean as when mother
rinsed them for Sunday
morning church.

We sing, find ways
to remember anew
what we had forgotten
when the world was new. ⫽

Send Us...

Send us a vinyl purist, a caretaker of good taste,
A Valhallan harmony singer, expert bomb defuser.

Patience long as cotton threads that tie us to a bobbin
moon,
backpockets overflowing with magicdust and kisses.

A traveller, cartographer, Indian ink spilling
glorious on the picture, smudging all the borders.

Archaeologist, cryptologist pinning up history lessons
on every school wall in the land, adults kept back for
detention.

A delectable chef, cooking spices from Chenzen,
pasta from Palermo, Parisienne puddings.

A brewer of mead, a fermenter of hope,
a repairer of sailcloths, a bonder of rope.

An urbane host for parties unpolitical,
a keeper of bunting and wishful secrets.

A bottomless inventor of universal panaceas,
a closer of mouths, and an opener of ears.

Send us ourselves on our most hopeful day
with the hope that we can be enough. ✍

From Peterloo to Tolpuddle

From Peterloo to Tolpuddle, Jarrow to Orgreave,
there'll be no further uprisings today sir,
we read the press, know what to believe.

The daily tales spin an almighty weave
about who's to blame, wouldn't you say sir
from Peterloo to Tolpuddle, Jarrow to Orgreave.

We've learned when to smile, when to grieve
and follow our orders like a precision tracer –
we read the press, know what to believe.

We kick out at the weak, the exposed and naive,
all those years of hate pointed the way sir,
from Peterloo to Tolpuddle, Jarrow to Orgreave.

So when our chance came, we ticked 'Leave',
seeing there was no alternative baser,
we read the press, know what to believe.

Ground ourselves into a corner with no reprieve,
we love our country so chose to disgrace her.
From Peterloo to Tolpuddle, Jarrow to Orgreave,
we read the press, know what to believe. ⁄⁄

Tale of the Riverbank

A brownness of gulls
patrol the river, dutybooks
tucked beneath their hulls,
pounding the beat, stern looks
arrowed at ramblers
picking through centuries.

Mid-poem, a lone salmon
slips its handlers,
leaps full-length from the water,
smashing through the meter and rhyme.
Breathe in this time. Return.
A pencil is a camera
for moments like these. ⁄⁄

Mr Byrne

He was great in lessons, Mr Byrne.
Softeyed, soft touch Deputy Head
who'd witnessed enough misery
to last six million lifetimes.

Easily distracted, led astray,
we'd throw him a line
and he'd draw it in the sand
just as the tide
was due to arrive.

Asif thirty years
was thirty seconds,
we'd be beckoned to Berlin,
where young Private Byrne
pickedup bits of broken buildings,
broken lives,
broken hearts,
rubbed them tender as tears
on a salt-starched tunic
until they soaked rightthrough his skin.

Now remember, boys and girls,
when times are tough, money tight,
blaming scapegoats is never right.
Great in lessons, Mr Byrne. ✍

The Ambling, the Dancing

Minute by hour, by day by year
we amble the land, soakup the sun
asif we had taken the winder
from the back of the clock,
put it in a favourite pocket,
like some buried underland
where all today's secrets
live out their halflives.

And we dance and we frolic
in the teeth of a sea devouring
the land beneath our feet.
Each sharpened grain of sand
tickling our toes is a tick;
as the sundial stays jailless,
ever unchanging, refusing
the prison of deepdark mines.

Regardless of our burying
and building and hiding,
our walls remain porous.
Time blows through the doors,
sandblasts our skin
and everything within it,
whispering through baddreams
I am beyond your control.

One by one we are pickedoff
remorseless. Rotted, broken,
roundbacked and thinboned,
until all we remember is
the ambling, the dancing,
the frolicking and soaking
in lovely, foolish days
of belief in foreverness. ∕∕

You Do Not Speak for Me

You do not speak for me.

The sparrow has my voice,
busying between hedgerows,
English as a cloudy day,
more English than you anyway.

That oldman and his dog,
out at dawn beachcombing,
letting the morning tickle
his mouth up at the edges,
his gait carries my weight
as he lightens the day.

The wildflowers on verges,
reaching for something
they can never quite touch,
but stretching all the same,
smudging their glories
allover the mundane.

These Saturday kids,
smiling through braces,
serving ice creams on days
when 'hot' doesn't cut it,
learning that patience is
waiting for sainted grandmas
to choose between
flake or sprinkles.

The policeman, the plumber,
the teacher, roadsweeper,
prampushing mums,
gleaming proud dads,

the Sunday funrunners
replenishing the sweat
with a pint of English best
after winning their bet.

The lifesaver doctor,
last hour of her shift
who hasn't slept since
God knows when;
as kindas kiss it betters
to the latest in a line
of confused oldladies all asking
'But where were you born dear?'
and 'Ooh what a lovely smile,
what lovely skin'
as she holds their hands,
asks them where it hurts.

This is my England.
Its voice is not scabrous,
it is soft.
Its fingers reach down
to pick up the fallen,
brushing them down,
to hold them aloft.

Your tone is shrill,
a study in antipathy.
You are not my England
and you do not speak for me. ⁄⁄

The Dreams of an Everyday Teenaged Boy

If I should see a rabbit
in the next five minutes
then the sky and all that's in it
can fall on me, I won't care,
for it means today is a good day.

And should I spy a squirrel
then the girl infront of me
in this queue for the 263
will turn and say she loves me,
because why wouldn't she?

But should I see a deer
I will know I'm still asleep
and the day ahead will creep
its seconds like hours
for no-one could be so lucky.

Thus meanders the time
in the early morning light
of the sunshine bus stop life
of an inbetween teenaged boy,
waiting for it all to start. //

Friday Night Rehearsal

A Friday night three, we,
standing in the doorway
of a stretchy weekend.
Close eyes, step through
to the fortune and fame
that we know,
we just know
is out there somewhere.

We run through our moves
like no one is watching,
like we were taught to.
Twirling between raindrops,
making a big splash,
loose paving stones
bowing beneath us.

We tell eachother I love you
and we do,
right here
right now
and that's all that matters.

Snugtogether in this
between showers cocoon
of a Friday night
where tomorrow is a doorway
to a life of dreams
for fourteen-year-old girls
who ripped their own jeans
just to fit through to tomorrow. ⁄⁄

Session

Somenights the jigs an' reels
take the beater from your fingers
and spin it round the room
like a dolly on acid
and the counting just happens,
comes through a window.

Somenights thirds an' fifths
are accompanied by sevenths
and the brethren gathered
all sup from the same glass,
which is misted with magic
and all the prophets hold dear.

And somenights, just somenights
tablelegs leave their station
and paddle in the joy
of a session gone native. ⁄⁄

Training

Down at the battery,
they're training patriots,
whizzbangs on the sand,
Land Of Hope And Glory.
The rattling of rounds,
fluffy pink bombs
and nobody dies.

No guts hanging out
drying in the breeze,
men who couldn't march a mile
kneel, fire caps
to cheering from
a brightblue morning crowd.

After the show, a queue.

Little boys just in school
line up at the army tent,
close cropped already.
Waiting. ⁄⁄

Desiderata

O build us a path
from cradle to grave,
one we can dance along,
singing *This is our song.*

With surface cut from turf
foundations forged in iron,
where women and men
stride into a future
worth more than money
and profits on walls.

And build us beds
made from soft landings
for days when our labours
tear at our temperance.

For we are worth more
than cogs in machines.
Our hearts keep time
with the turning of seasons,
our hands help the fallen
back onto their feet
and we carry eachother
when our bodies fail us.

So build us a path
deep and wide and long,
for this is our land
and this is our song. ⫽

New Town, Old Story

Against a tattered backdrop curtain
of bandit machines, Penny falls.
Glitter ripped from the sundown town,
she careers her teary gin dance.

Pinballing from bollards to chipvan,
limbs loose as ringpulls on the wind.

Some lives are hard and that is all. ⁄⁄

Sing

We sing as an imperative,
we do because we must.
With music we are nightingales,
without it we are rust.
Like the faces of flowers
incline towards the sun,
so we are all an inch taller
with music's constant hum.
And when indeed we find a voice,
one that rings in our own head,
the heart inside beats afresh,
the soul around it newly fed.
When asked *Why do you sing?*
Answer *Doesn't everything?* ⁄⁄

Secret

It's a secret he said, *nobody must know*
and so she sewed her lips closed
with whisky and Golden Virginia,
held her nose and inhaled her future.

A secret that stays within these walls.
A gesture towards missing floorboards,
home to a tangle of shadows and spiders,
where mum and dad would never find her.

So she saved up her secrets
and stubbed them in ashtrays,
a thousand sharp, dark brown burns
on pure virgin crystal glass,
breathing out the Teachers
to show what she had learned. ⁄⁄

Imago

What will you do when we're gone boys and girls,
what will you do when we're gone?
All we beasties and bugs,
creepy crawlies and slugs,
o what will you do when we're gone?

What if the swallows don't come back next year,
what if the swallows don't come?
No more swooping the air
for food that's not there,
o what if the swallows don't come?

What will you eat without bees boys and girls,
what will you eat without bees?
All the flowers and plants
don't only feed ants.
No pollen, nor honey?
No food in your tummy!
O what will you eat without bees?

What shall we bequeath our grandchildren now,
what shall we leave for them now?
A sour cup to sup
as their planet heats up,
the consequence of
the tidal wave of love
we left in our will –
o what a bitter pill!
That's what we'll leave for them now. ⁄⁄

A Warming Lullaby

Mummy look, the moon is on fire!
Don't worry my darling, my love,
my sweet.
It's only the sandman's
padding feet, creeping away
back to the clouds' crimson crib.

Mummy look, the blanket's ablaze!
Don't fret my pet, my poppet,
my honey.
Your head has gone light,
your tummy feels funny
from this shortage of air.
The CO2 has tomorrow set fair
as it twinkles bright in our lungs.

Mummy look, my toys are melting!
Don't be silly my petal, my pearldrop,
my dear.
That last wave took your sister,
our neighbours, your friends,
but I'll stay here with you
until the very end.
I've shuttered the windows,
locked all the doors.
Now two heads, one pillow
        two heads, one pillow. ✍

A Frayed Reassurance

Do not be afraid of ghosts my darling,
the graveyards keep tighthold of old bones
and Newton's Third Law has your back,
a hand pushing us away from foolish superstition.

Don't not be afraid of the dark my lovely,
it is only the daylight run out of puff,
the sun is having a snooze is all
(do not look this bit up in your science book).

Never Go Home

You town of a thousand mouths,
all coughing up the sulphur,
Warner's chimney a middle finger
to sticky little questions,
like *Why is the river yellowgreen?*
and *Where have all the fish gone?*

You den of drunken husbands,
all teaching their children
Don't get above your station,
nor harbour any dreams at all,
for that's the way of the world
when it ends in your backyard.

You nursery to brutes, who
learned well that slapped faces,
slapped arses, slapped legs
never did them any harm
as they keenly pass on
The Wisdom Of The Whack
to their own little loves
in the University Of Life,
still openly smoking
behind the bike sheds.

You bonfire of tomorrows
with your blackened backstreets,
I will throw you off
like pissdamp bedsheets,
knowing you'll soak back in
through the pores of the night,
when your sons and daughters,
blown on the winds,
still dream of bridge building
but can never go home again. ⁄⁄

Bluesky Thinking

Bluesky thinking took my cares away,
cleaned the scores from my knuckles,
eased the padding from my knees,
left coal drowned in blackened ground,
steel cold on the rolls in eggshell hellholes,
those blood orange monuments
to who we once were.

Bluesky thinking took my savings away,
a goodcause donation to merchant bankers
in lieu of the tax they nolonger pay.
A postbox in the Cayman Islands
goes an awful long way
in a world turned upside down.

Bluesky thinking took my children away
to factory farmlands of headsets and screens,
plugged into the mainstream, their dreams
subsumed into walls fullof targets,
where they have to put their hands up
to empty their bladders.

Bluesky thinking took all their horizons
and painted them vulgar onto talent shows.
"I'm a nonentity, get me a life!
I'm helpful, obedient and give off no flak".
Bluesky thinking turned the skies black. ⁂

Instructions for Would-Be Poets

Fill your head with reading
then forget every single word.
Shut out all distractions
but keep them on a lead.

Try not to talk in metaphors
then surprise yourself with one.
Fit your pictures in a mirror.
Throw a breezeblock at it.

Find your voice, then shout
until it sounds like someone else.
Keep breaking it until it limps
back home with new rough edges.

You don't have to use quatrains,
poetry is not all 4/4 time,
but do it anyway. Throw in
an annoying, obvious rhyme.

Make a note to edit out
that offending verse later
but deliberately keep it in,
just out of bad, like.

Know your own Hinterland,
feed it with time and love.
When folk ask where poems come from
say they fall from the skies
or grow wild on unruly stanzas.
Believe your own lies.

Train your toes to grip the tightrope
between pleasing the reader

and pleasing yourself.
Pretend you have a reader.
Fall off. Revel in the mess
of all that spilled ink.

Keep doing it.

And should someone set out do's and don'ts,
holy rules of this's and that's,
roll them up into a mental ball,
apply lighter fluid and strike a match. ⁄⁄

Surf's Up

I went to the beach,
called out to the shuggyboats.
Their guttering gurgles
bubbled up through foam,
We are drowned,
gone down with the donkeys
and kissmequick hats.

I went to the river
with a hotline to the water,
but all I saw
was a bobbity fish,
its plastic guts
and a look that spoke
of a longtime dead.

I went back to the land,
its butchered wounds packed
with pretty putrefaction.
It's bigmouth flopped open,
all rottenteeth and tincans
and roared a tsunami home. ⁄⁄

Doorstepping / Goosestepping

Here they come, those Fourth Reich sons,
banging on my windows and doors.
They say they only want to talk
but I can hear them shouting, shouting.

They came a-pounding undercover of night,
rattling glass loose from its frame.
They say their fists are openwide
but I can hear them hammering, hammering.

I have called the police station,
to the sound of crying child and wife.
They say no crime has been committed
and I can hear them laughing, laughing.

The police came, the gang dispersed,
saying I should learn to keep schtum.
They say that they'll be back again
and I can hear them marching, marching. ⁄⁄

Love in Winter

She sends him kisses with his pills
every boneache morning,
he returns them in the rubbing
of her bunioned feet.

It's in the peeling of potatoes,
the scrubbing of the pans,
kindness in the silence,
the odd squeeze of a hand.

It's in the relinquishing of pride,
the sharing of high ground,
the reaching up to high shelves
twice weekly in Poundland.

It's in the topping up of tea,
the mug not yet half drained,
knowing how she takes her tea –
milk in first, and strained.

It's in the venturing outdoors
whenever they are able,
the helping on of hats and coats
and the tucking in of labels.

Each tut he makes is a hand round her waist
and if he squints she is twenty one,
as she sends her love in lectures
beneath a dipping Winter sun. ✐

Goodnight from Mars

You must have known
when you sent me off
that you had built an orphan.
A slave to science
who you would strand
and when the time came,
abandon.

All these thoughts and deeds,
unanswered messages,
home thoughts from abroad,
from the land
of tracks and burrows
and cold, dead rock.

I always knew
this day would come.
Programme-perfect
and right on cue,
you play me a song
by one more of your orphans,
scorched like earth
by your distant love.

Farewell then my father,
my traitor, my God.
From this moment on
I only look down. ⁄⁄

Whisperfish

I am Whisperfish.
I will not be rushed out
into the broadblack,
fin-backed, scabrous sea
of some cackhanded,
wayward diver's dream.

I will wait instead
in the shade of this rock,
cool water strumming
its airless guitarstrings,
a softas snow lullaby
to rock-a-bye hiders.

I will metamorphose
in my own largo time,
soft but insistent,
tapping, tapping
until the beat
belongs only to me.

I am Whisperfish
and my voice,
for so long a zephyr,
is a song of Summer
and my lips' parting
sweeps leaves from trees. ✍

Advice to Children

Do not stare at the sun,
it still has the feathers
from your father's back
as a scalp and a slap
for wantful daydreaming.

Do not follow the stars,
they are not a still canvas
but a whirligig reel,
breathless and raging
to dazzle you blind.

The plough turns no fields,
it sits empty and dry,
a panhandle pointing
to a corner of the sky
where Greek myths go to die.

If you leap high enough
you cannot catch the moon,
but you can hold its glow
in the heart of your coat
to see you home safe on dark days. ⫽

Commence the Dancing...

A tip of the hat
to a soft-shoe shuffle
and silly old boys
up to no good atall
outside saloon doors.

A ruffle of babyhair
to fussy fat fingers
tenderly correcting
an errant manchild's
tie gone askew.

A cheek-to-cheek tango
to teary faces
and the wafer-thin line
between laughing and crying
and how it takes a fool
to know the difference. ✐

Dot....dot....dot....

Astronomers have revealed details of mysterious signals emanating from a distant galaxy, picked up by a telescope in Canada. Among the 13 fast radio bursts, known as FRBs, was a very unusual repeating signal, coming from the same source about 1.5 billion light years away.
BBC World Service, 10 January 2019

A dot inside a galaxy
is tapdancing radio waves
at a blue speck of dust
from a billion lightyears
safe in the distance.

An encoded How do you do?
to a squabbling monkey world
that has unshakeable beliefs
in pixie dust but laughs at
veracity square in the face.

Take your electronic kisses elsewhere friend,
there is no welcome for you here.
Put your longarmed hugs on hold,
a half-life of fifteen minutes, however bold,
is not worth all that lovely pulsing. ⁄⁄

Boiling a Frog

The revolution is being televised,
we're all gluedfast to our sofas,
choked on smoke, dazzled by mirrors,
while on the street the loafers
are frozen in their sleeping bags.

We create our facebook memes,
such clever, vacant nonsense:
modernday snake oil creams
to ease an aching conscience
about shop doorway piles of rags.

Meanwhile everyone's happy
online shopping's ever-cheaper
while the foodbank queues
grow colder and deeper,

never wondering for a moment
about the shuttered shopfronts,
nor the people who served us
whose families bore the brunt

of our foul and fickle blindness.
Workers begging at warehouses
for their zero-hour scraps
at the behest of our browsers.

And now the military forces
are readying for the streets
as we dither and worry,
issue sadface tweets.

Dissatisfied and distracted
by news drizzling down on us,
as degree by degree water
heats up around us. ⟆

Waiting for the Swallows' Return

A tiny spear cast from Africa,
two hundred miles a day
on the wild, wild wind,
they are almost here now.

A blueblack beaked heartbeat's
flash will pitch up in
the very same eaves
of the very same building
in the very same village
where they breathed their first.

Each Pyrenean backpacker
travelling light, a dart
straight into the heart of a nation
who needs newcomers
like a smallbird needs food
and a peaceful corner. ⁄⁄

Midmorning Springtown

Miniature buggy pushers,
mummy's little helpers
are cornering the racetrack
of the sunspeckled terraces,
their Formula 1 passengers
asleep behind the wheel
in midmorning Springtown.

Dogs walk their owners,
plundering playingfields
for piratical treasures,
long tossed overboard
by some pegleg captain
dreaming his way home
from primary school.

Tabby cats board doorsteps,
whiskers twitching with dreams
of the mouse who got away
and how that flashy finch
on number 44's fence
will end up in the gutter
one fine night.

The railway bridge hums
to the run of the wheels
of the 10.34 flier,
arms reaching for the wire,
powering its passengers
as they peer out at buggies,
babies' dropped dummies,
their sisters and brothers,
list-busying mothers,
cats and dogs

up to no-good plotting
in the picture-perfect
of midmorning Springtown
come alive in the sun. ⁄⁄

Echoes

We tip-tappy down
these hushquiet streets
in an out of season town,
the sun hiding shy behind
its cloudy accomplice,
the lesser walked paths
still nursing the echoes
of lobster-potting fishwives
and their latenight talk
over candlelit nets,
needles and knuckles,
ganseys and fishhooks;
of catching the tide,
change coming on the wind
and how nowt lasts forever
but somedays if you stop,
squeeze your breath tight
as a bulging basket
you can catch yesterday,
alive and bright silver
dancing like a mackerel
on a fisherman's best line. ⁄⁄

What We Have Become

Meet me by moonlight
on the sailors' trod,
that path made black
by what filled the bellies
of our mums and dads.

We'll walk on the bones
of riveters' catchers,
fitters and their mates
who built a world's bridges
but themselves couldn't escape
so instead slung them 'cross rivers
and stuck out their hands
to bid welcome to strangers.

Take the black path past
the BOS plant, Beam Mill,
where nightshift ghosts
play cards in the messroom,
their pennies spotwelded
to the rust-holed table.

Then back to the docks
still laden with ships,
sailors pounding a trod
to the Captain Cook
for tabs and a skinful
and a roll in the sawdust.

Meet me under moonlight
and we'll scare ourselves dumb
not with talltales of yore
but by what we have become. ⟋

Not Rain

It's not rain,
it's Venus wringing out
her locks over the sea,
the clouds her bath towels.

It's not rain,
it's tears from
the moon's sorry face,
who feels every smidge
of the slowly growing distance
from her blue eyed partner.

It's not rain,
it's a planet's retribution
on the saw-handed apes
marauding through the trees,
backpockets fat with fivers
from ministers and newsmen.

It's not rain,
it's the synchronised splashing
of Busby Berkeley's ghosts,
falling down to order,
a cheap B-movie distraction,
the audience clapping wildly
at the choreographed action.

It's not rain,
it's a signpost,
letters painted in red.
Something about
a coming tsunami.
It sinks beneath the water
unseen,
unread. ⫽

Song of the Six Million

It didn't begin with uniform wearers,
armband bearers, that's just where it ended,
with proud keyholders to blandly
wicked gas chambers.

It started on the streets, in the shops
and bars, with late night whispers
and jokes about the Jews and who's
to blame for all the ills of the day.

It was carried along like a smile,
like a song by the middle-of-the-roaders,
the go-with-the-flow-ers,
the deaf, dumb and blind
and the want-a-quiet-lifers.

And no-one really noticed
unless they were called Cohen,
or Meyer or Levin or Stein
but everybody knew
about the over-sensitive Jews,
touchy and greedy
and have you ever noticed
how they don't look like us?

And so like a snowball in winter
it rolled merrily along,
like a smile, like a song,
this wonderful new truth
that would make the nation strong,
this great Fatherland
with its old ways and new,
a promised land for all –
well, all but the Jew.

It didn't start with Panzers
rampaging through Paris,
nor ghettos, nor mass graves,
children cowering in attics.

No human skin lampshades
in the fabled masterplan,
but call people sub-human
and yourself Superman,
and it's only going one way.

Down a dead-end street
where grandmas and grandads,
aunties and uncles, half-starved children
and their mums and dads
are lined up against a wall,
the lucky ones spared
a last train ride to a death camp
nestled in the countryside.

Their voices ghost out
from bulletholed walls,
from obscene trenches,
from railtracks leading
to Arbeit Macht Frei,
a laughable legacy
from a sick joke world.

Six million strangled battlecries
to beware ignorance and fear:
*We too thought
it could never happen here.* ⁒

'Unskilled'

She is not unskilled,
she is full of humanity,
she deals with it daily –
the blood and shit of life
in all its dark glory.

She is particularly good
at holding the hand of your mum,
who doesn't know you anymore,
who cries in the night
for a hug from her daddy
long cold in the ground.

She has a degree in There There,
performed in sing song
at four in the morning
while changing wet sheets
and making it better.

Her cloak of invisibility,
an unwanted superpower,
renders her open to attack
from gladhanding climbers
on their way upwards
to nowhere special,
greasing the pole behind them.

She has diplomas in kindness,
patience and back breaking work,
to the background noise
of the sneers and smears of some jerk
who wouldn't have the balls
to do her job.

She is as skilled as magicians.
Her body is the foundry
of a nation suddenly grateful,
her heart its steel press;
if she falls, we all fall.

She is powered by thanks
and a job well done,
the pacified pulse
of a heart gone haywire.

She is he, is husband, midwife,
cleaner, nurse, care giver, osteopath
and she stands as mighty as a forest
as she carries us all on her back. ✍

Island

How can you say
we are bigger and better
when we are
a pinprick
of blood on a map?

Scarlet fingerprints,
smeared like oil
in the name
of the queen
and civilisation.

We drawbridge pullers,
dulling our senses
with patriot songs,
fingers in ears.

Denying that islands
are sunk when the tide
inexorably rises. ⁄⁄

Happy Yet?

i.m. Jo Cox

So there is blood upon the street.
Hatred's vein has slit a servant,
vented its bile onto black tarmac.

As the gimlet-eyed ring master,
taking lessons from the fuhrer,
unveils his identikit Nazi cartoon.

We Anglo-Saxon sons and daughters
watch as England's wasted youth
smash up our neighbours' cafes.

The nation who wrote
the world's history books
has plainly forgotten how to read.

Are we happy yet? ⁄⁄

Meeting Male Audience Members After Poetry Readings

Reading between the lines,
a pattern is emerging
around words and their meanings,
the rendering of feelings.

Somewhere between English and Maths
and schooltrips to the baths
there were obviously lessons
long expelled from my memory.

Perhaps the girls were doing
home economics or shorthand
or queueing to jump into
the stereotyping pool.

But somewhere in timetable land,
slotted in sly as a rib dig
must have been a sticky hour a week
on The Unmanly Shame Of Poetry.

Techniques including lip curling,
confused face, shrugs and open scorn
were crammed like emotions
into a metalwork vice.

I see them all now,
the blushing old boys,
sitting neatly in rows,
clandestine wives for cover.

Studiously straightfaced,
not a stiff lip out of place.
Then afterwards, stealthy as

a nightshift worker,
with everyone else
hidden safely from sight,
they cross the shopfloor.

Sidling up, the sly old dogs,
eyes puddling, they shrug
and tell me tersely
(just between me and them, like)

Smashing that, mate... ⁄⁄

The Queen of Lost Things

She is the queen of lost things
misplacer of the everyday;
earrings, brushes, pencils, pens
sleek their way into strategically
placed wormholes,
magically reappearing
for a months later encore.

The house sings along daily
to her wonderment refrains
of gleeful *there you ares*
and *I wondered where that was.*

One day she found
a tattered old lost boy.
She applied spit and polish
and decided to keep him
as treasure. ✍

The God of Perfect Things

I am the God of Perfect Things
and I give you
your father's fixit hands,
his methodical brain,
his temperament, patientas tools
forged in a flame
long before you were born.
His tin of swarfega
that never quite took
the oilmarks from fingertips,
those fingerprint woodblocks
for which he would naturally
knockup the frame
from bits hanging off
the ordered garage walls.

I am the Goddess of Domesticity
and I give you
perfect pies plucked from the steam
of a neveroff oven,
to feed the openhouse
of outstretched palms,
bellies hungryas
nestling cuckoo chicks,
who sleptin soft cotton sheets
and dreamt the dreams
of the needless.

I am God's Removal Man.
On days like these I take
this sepia from your shoulders,
grown heavy as
lead framed looking-glass,
and let you also recall

the splinters that strayed
under his nails
and the language that came with them,
the moments she was wordless, copeless;
the silences between them
and the knowledge that perfection
is the harshest of targets. ⫽

We Are Each Other

We need a brother of the blues;
come blow your horn, light a fuse
beneath the tinder of our fickle
lie-down-and-take-it,
ever-so-humble,
bowing, scraping days.

We need Sister Rosetta
to rasp and wake us better,
shake our crumbling foundations
and hold us up a mirror,
come deliver us from ourselves.

We need to relearn to sing,
find our voices again
til our harmonies ring
as discords loosen the cement
of the walls that hold us in.

We need an old preacher man
clad in rags and frays,
come bearing brush and pan,
help clear up the mess we've made,
pick up the sisters and brothers
who tumbled to the gutter
while we looked the other way.

We need a singer from the choir,
with a voice of sand and honey,
carrying the truth like a torchsong
until like children we sing along:

We are each other!
We are each other! //

Other anthologies and collections available from Stairwell Books

Iconic Tattoo	Richard Harries
Fatherhood	CS Fuqua
Herdsmenization	Ngozi Olivia Osuoha
On the Other Side of the Beach, Light	Daniel Skyle
Words from a Distance	Ed. Amina Alyal, Judi Sissons
All My Hands Are Now Empty	Linda Baker
Fractured	Shannon O'Neill
Unknown	Anna Rose James, Elizabeth Chadwick Pywell
When We Wake We Think We're Whalers from Eden	Bob Beagrie
Awakening	Richard Harries
Geography Is Irrelevant	Ed. Rose Drew, Amina Alyal, Raef Boylan
Belong	Ed. Verity Glendenning, Stephanie Venn, Amy E Creighton
Starspin	Graehame Barrasford Young
Out of the Dreaming Dark	Mary Callan
A Stray Dog, Following	Greg Quiery
Blue Saxophone	Rosemary Palmeira
Steel Tipped Snowflakes 1	Izzy Rhiannon Jones, Becca Miles, Laura Voivodeship
Where the Hares Are	John Gilham
The Glass King	Gary Allen
A Thing of Beauty Is a Joy Forever	Don Walls
Gooseberries	Val Horner
Poetry for the Newly Single 40 Something	Maria Stephenson
Northern Lights	Harry Gallagher
Nothing Is Meant to be Broken	Mark Connors
Heading for the Hills	Gillian Byrom-Smith
More Exhibitionism	Ed. Glen Taylor
The Beggars of York	Don Walls
Lodestone	Hannah Stone
Unsettled Accounts	Tony Lucas
Learning to Breathe	John Gilham
New Crops from Old Fields	Ed. Oz Hardwick
The Ordinariness of Parrots	Amina Alyal
Somewhere Else	Don Walls
Still Life with Wine and Cheese	Ed. Rose Drew, Alan Gillott
Taking the Long Way Home	Steve Nash

For further information please contact rose@stairwellbooks.com
www.stairwellbooks.co.uk
@stairwellbooks

Ingram Content Group UK Ltd.
Milton Keynes UK
UKHW010217100523
421505UK00002B/12